THERE'S NO WRONG WAY TO PRAY

By Rebecca Ninke and Kate E.H. Watson

Illustrated by Liam Darcy

beaming books

MINNEAPOLIS

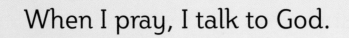

When I pray, I talk to God.

I tell God about my goldfish,
living or floating.

I pray for the kids at school.

Even the naughty ones.

Especially the naughty
ones who sit by me.

I pray when I'm afraid.

When an ambulance goes by with lights on, I pray for whoever is waiting for it to arrive.

I pray before I eat.

Unless I'm really hungry.

Then I pray after I eat.

Sometimes I pray when I'm in the bathroom, especially if I forgot a book.

I'll even pray when I'm riding my bike or rollerblading,

especially when I'm going downhill.

I pray when I'm doing my chores,

even when I'm picking up dog poop.

I hope God doesn't mind.

I pray for my dog because he can't go to church.

If he did, he'd run around and knock over the candles and eat the communion wafers.

I pray for my cat, but she just stares at me.

I tried to play baptism with her once,

but then I had to pray for my scratches to heal.

I pray for people I don't know.

The ones I hear about on the news.

I pray for people who
live where life is hard.

BREAKING NEWS: TORNADO

And it helps me remember it's no biggie when the Wi-Fi is out or my brother eats my Halloween candy.

I used to pray that my team would win.

But then I wondered if the other team prayed for that too.

That must put God in a difficult situation.

Now I just pray that no one gets hurt.

I pray for my family.
And my grandma in heaven.

I wonder if God
nods her way
when I do,
and then she
smiles.

I pray for weird stuff sometimes.

The bug I accidentally stepped on who wasn't looking so good later.

The kid at the store who was having a tantrum.

The teenager with purple hair and a nose ring.

My mom prays for his mom too.

I pray for the whole earth and all the animals living on it.

I pray for places I've never seen.

People I'll never meet.

I like to think they pray for me too.

Sometimes I pray for things that are more like wishes.

Once I prayed I would get a unicorn for Christmas.

My mom prayed that her eyes wouldn't get stuck that way.

Then we forgot to pray for a while because we were laughing so hard.

I bet God was laughing too.

Nighttime is my best time to pray.

It's dark and my mom is sitting beside me.

My dog is on the floor focused on loud personal hygiene.

My cat is on the bed, snoring.

My mom and I end our prayers the same way most nights:

Give all the children food to eat,

A place to sleep

And someone to love and protect them.

Amen.

When I pray, I talk to God—

wherever I am, whatever I'm doing, whoever I'm with.

I used to believe there was only one right way to pray.

But now I think there's no wrong way to pray.

Text copyright © 2019 Rebecca Ninke and Kate E.H. Watson
Illustration copyright © 2019 Beaming Books

Published in 2019 by Beaming Books, an imprint of 1517 Media. All rights reserved. No part of this book may be
reproduced without the written permission of the publisher. Email copyright@1517.media. Printed in the USA.

25 24 23 22 21 20 19   1 2 3 4 5 6 7 8

ISBN: 978-1-5064-4932-6

Library of Congress Cataloging-in-Publication Data
Names: Ninke, Rebecca, author. | Watson, Kate E. H., author. | Darcy, Liam,
    illustrator.
Title: There's no wrong way to pray / written by Rebecca Ninke and Kate E.H.
    Watson ; illustrated by Liam Darcy.
Other titles: There is no wrong way to pray
Description: First edition. | Minneapolis, MN : Beaming Books, 2019. |
    Summary: A child reflects on prayer, including different ways to pray,
    things to pray for, and times to pray, ranging from silly, wish-like
    prayers at Christmas to nightly prayers for all children to be fed,
    sheltered, and loved.
Identifiers: LCCN 2018030772 | ISBN 9781506449326 (hard cover : alk. paper)
Subjects: | CYAC: Prayer--Fiction. | God--Fiction.
Classification: LCC PZ7.1.N58 The 2019 | DDC [E]--dc23 LC record available at https://lccn.loc.gov/2018030772

VN0004589;9781506447728;DEC2018

Beaming Books
510 Marquette Avenue
Minneapolis, MN 55402
Beamingbooks.com